P9-APJ-545

CCJC

How Artists View Weather

Karen Hosack

Heinemann Library
Chicago, Illinois

Customer Service 888-454-2279
Visit our website at www.heinemannlibrary.com

Designed by Ron Kamen and Celia Floyd
Illustrations by Jo Brooker
Originated by Dot Gradations Ltd
Printed and bound in China by South China Printing
Company

09 08 07 06 05
10 9 8 7 6 5 4 3 2 1

Library of Congress Cataloging-in-Publication Data

Hosack, Karen.
  Weather / Karen Hosack.
    v. cm. -- (How artists view)
  Includes index.
  Contents: How artists see weather -- Simple pictures --
Lines and dashes -- Cool colors -- The big freeze -- Warm
colors -- On the beach -- Sketching the weather -- Shapes
and patterns -- Patterns and movement -- Whipping up a
storm -- Painting the power of nature -- Weather as people.
  ISBN 1-4034-4855-8
  1. Weather in art--Juvenile literature. 2. Art--Juvenile
literature. [1. Weather in art. 2. Art appreciation.] I. Title.
  N8261.W42H67 2004
  704.9'43--dc22
                                        2003026364

Acknowledgments

The author and publisher are grateful to the following for
permission to reproduce copyright material:

Alamy Images p. 13 top; Ancient Art and Architecture
Collection Ltd p. 28 top; BBC Photographic Library p. 6;
Bridgeman Art Library pp. 4 (Musée d'Orsay, Paris), 12
(Rijksmuseum, Amsterdam), 16 (The National Gallery), 18
(Ashmolean Museum, Oxford), 19 (The National Gallery),
20 (Stadtische Galerie im Lenbachhaus, Munich), 25
(Kunstalle, Hamburg), 27 (The Nolde Foundation,
Germany); © Bridget Riley, 2004 p. 22 (All rights reserved /
Private collection, London / courtesy Karsten Schubert,
London); Carnegie Museum of Art, Pittsburgh p. 24
(Howard N. Eavenson Memorial Collection); © Cleveland
Museum of Art p. 15 (Mr and Mrs William H. Marlatt Fund,
1965.233); Corbis pp. 5 (Richard T. Nowitz), 7; © 2004
Cordon Art B.V. – Baarn-Holland p. 21 (All rights reserved);
National Gallery, London pp. 10, 28 bottom; Ohara
Museum of Art, Japan p. 9 (© ADAGP, Paris and DACS,
London 2004); Philadelphia Museum of Art p. 11; Philips
Collection p. 8 (© ADAGP, Paris and DACS, London 2004);
Snowman Enterprises Ltd p. 13 bottom; Statens Museum for
Kunst, Copenhagen p. 14; Tate London 2004 p. 26; Tudor
Photography pp. 17 x 3, 23 x 3, 29.

Cover photograph (*Tidal Wave* by Liz Wright, 1983)
reproduced with permission of Bridgeman Art Library
(Private collection).

Every effort has been made to contact copyright holders of
any material reproduced in this book. Any omissions will be
rectified in subsequent printings if notice is given to the
publisher.

Some words are shown
in bold, **like this.** You
can find out what they
mean by looking in the
glossary.

Contents

How Artists See Weather

When the sun shines we feel warm and happy and want to be outdoors. In the winter, when it is cold, we have to dress in warm clothes. Many artists enjoy exploring weather, and how it makes us feel. Here

Renoir has shown sunlight using white dabs of paint. The patchy patterns on the ground also appear on the people's clothes. The sun is shining through the trees. The light seems to move with the swaying leaves.

The Swing by Pierre-Auguste Renoir, 1876

This snowy photograph could be printed on a holiday card. The scene reminds us of a cold, crisp winter morning. It must have only just stopped snowing because there are no footprints.

Simple Pictures

People like to know what the weather will be like. They want to know if the sidewalks and roads will be icy or if their boats will be tossed around on a stormy sea. To find out about the weather we look at a **weather forecast.** You can find these in newspapers, on the television, and on the **Internet.** These reports use pictures to make it easy to see what the weather is going to be like. We call these pictures **symbols.**

Symbols of weather can also be found in **Aboriginal** art:

This symbol means rain

This symbol means lightning

This symbol means a rainbow

The Aboriginal culture can be traced back to **prehistoric** times in Australia. Some of the symbols Aboriginal people use today in their paintings are the same as those found in caves that were painted thousands of years ago.

Aboriginal painting from Uluru (once known as Ayer's Rock), Australia.

Lines and Dashes

Both of the artists on these pages have used simple lines and dashes to show rain. In Braque's painting, the rain is only on one side of the tree as the shower passes by. The white lines are broken up to form dashes, giving us the feeling that the rain is not very heavy.

The Shower by Georges Braque, 1952

The **background** in this painting
is quite dark. It looks like a stormy
black cloud. The lines of rain are
streaked on the canvas, sometimes
crossing over each other. The rain
is very heavy.

Cold Colors

Blue and green make us feel cold. They remind us of the deep sea. This winter scene in Finland makes us feel chilly. The shafts of ice on the blue water show that the weather is freezing. Some of the white paint has been put on the canvas very thickly. This is called **impasto.** It has been streaked across the painting to look like watery reflections.

Lake Keitele by Akseli Gallen-Kallela, 1905

10

River Early Morning by
Camille Pissarro, 1888

This is a very cold early morning scene just before
the sun has warmed the air. We can see the yellow
flickers of sun on the water, but the main colors in
the painting are blues and white. Pissarro creates the
misty effect by using small dashes of paint. This makes
it look foggy.

A Big Freeze

Winter Scene with Skaters by a Windmill by Hendrick Avercamp, around 1615

In this painting, the dark shapes of the people's bodies stand out against the white ice and sky. If you look very closely, you can see what games people liked to play in the winter about 400 years ago. We can see people sledding, skating, and holding sticks to play a game like ice hockey.

The **sculpture** on the right is made out of ice. The artist would have had to work quickly before the ice had a chance to melt. By using materials from nature, the artist has shown how people can make beautiful things without damaging the **environment.**

The Snowman
This character is from a children's book titled *The Snowman*, by Raymond Briggs. The **illustration** is rounded and slightly fuzzy, making it look dream-like.

Warm Colors

Red, orange, and yellow make us feel hot. When artists want to put heat in their work they use **warm colors.** This painting shows a warm summer day. The sun shines through the vine leaves that grow around the wooden frame of a garden **pergola.** The artist has highlighted the sun on the leaves and dabbed warm yellows and shades of orange on the stone floor.

A Pergola by Christoffer Wilhelm Eckersberg, 1813–1816

Twilight in the Wilderness by
Fredric Edwin Church, 1860

The sun is setting in the evening twilight in this
painting. Strong bright colors contrast with the
darkness of the sky. The warm red reminds us of the
old saying "Red sky at night shepherd's delight, red
sky in the morning shepherd's warning." From this
saying, what do you think the weather was like the
day after this sunset was painted?

On the Beach

Monet enjoyed painting outdoors. He painted this beach scene when he was on vacation with his family. The weather must have been very hot because he has chosen to paint with warm colors. It might also have been a windy day, because sand from the beach has blown into the paint!

The Beach at Trouville by Claude Monet, 1870

Paint your own seaside scene

You will need:

- *paint and paintbrushes*
- *paper*
- *some sand*
- *a **palette** for mixing your paint*

Instructions:

1. Use your palette to mix the paints you will use for your painting. As well as blues for the sea and sky, you could use warm red, orange, and yellow to give your picture a sunny, summery feel.

2. Give your picture a "painted outdoors" look by mixing some sand into the paint on your palette. You could use this sandy paint for the beach! The sand will also give your picture **texture.**

3. You should now have your own sandy seaside scene!

Sketching the Weather

John Constable enjoyed painting outdoors. He would lie on his back and paint clouds in different weather conditions. Next to his oil painting sketches like the one below, he would write the date, time, and notes about the weather. Later, back in his **studio,** he would use these records of the weather to help him paint larger paintings like the one on page nineteen.

Study of Clouds by John Constable, around 1822

This painting was done in a studio. In real life it is much bigger than the painting on page eighteen. To help him, the artist would have used many sketches of clouds and rainbows, as well as of the cathedral and horses. Rainbows appear when the sun shines through rain droplets. Constable shows the dark clouds and bright sun which would have created the ideal conditions for a rainbow to appear.

Salisbury Cathedral from the Meadows by John Constable, around 1831–1834

Shapes and Patterns

This picture shows Franz Marc, his wife, and his dog caught in a downpour of rain. The red and yellow streaks make the rain look warm. As we look through the rain the figures are jagged and broken up. These patterns make it difficult to see the people and dog at first. In which direction do you think the rain is blowing?

In the Rain by Franz Marc, 1912

Rippled Surface by Maurits
Cornelis Escher, 1950

Maurits Escher did not need to use much detail in this
picture. The movement is shown perfectly by the
simple black and white shapes. Droplets of rain have
fallen from the branches of a tree onto this pond. We
can see the tree reflected in the water. The ringed
patterns are growing bigger and bigger until, in a
moment, the water will again be still and flat.

Patterns and Movement

This pattern seems to move when we look at it. This style of painting is called Op Art because it is an optical illusion. This means that it tricks the eye in to seeing something that is not really there. Bridget Riley named this piece *Shiver*. This could be because it reminded her of wind blowing across a pond. It could also be because the pattern shivers, just like we do if we are outside when it is cold.

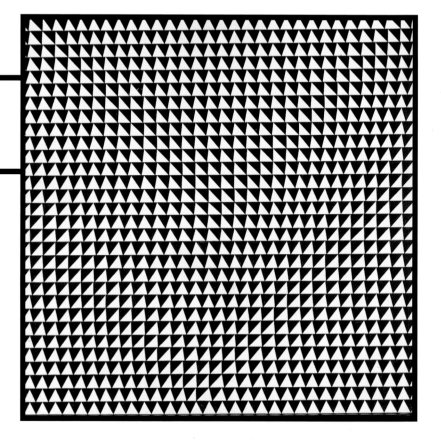

Shiver by
Bridget Riley,
1964

Make your own weather patterns using lines and shapes

You will need:

- *some paper*
- *colored pencils, felt-tip markers, or paint*

Instructions:

1. First, use your pencils, felt-tip markers, or paint to draw lots of different marks on a large sheet of paper. Next, look at the marks you have made and see if any remind you of different types of weather. For example, you might think that a swirly scribble reminds you of a storm.

2. Now try making a picture showing a type of weather using just simple lines and shapes. Use **cold colors** for winter weather, and **warm colors** for summer weather. If you cannot decide what to draw, you could try using simple lines and shapes to draw a hail storm, a windy day, or a warm breeze.

3 You should now have your finished weather pattern picture!

Whipping Up a Storm

We can see that the clouds in this painting are heavy with rain and a storm is about to start. Just before a big storm the sky goes very dark. To give the painting a **dramatic effect,** the artist has lit the dark sky on one side. You can almost hear the thunder in the background.

Thunderstorm at the Shore by Martin Johnson Heade, around 1870–1871

This man is standing on the edge of some rocks, looking out toward some misty mountains in the distance. The mountains are faint and smaller than the rocks the man is standing on. This is called **perspective**. This means they look further away than the objects in the **foreground** of the painting.

Painting the Power of Nature

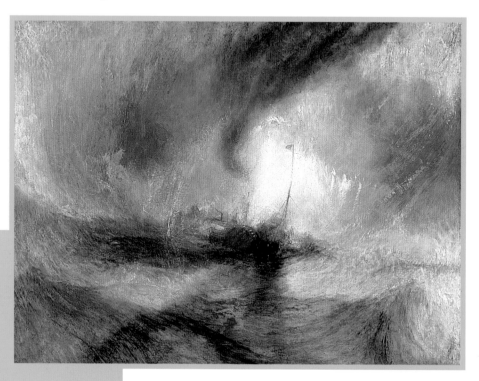

Snow Storm
by Joseph
Turner, 1842

Joseph Turner enjoyed going out in stormy weather. He used those experiences to create paintings back in his **studio.** This is a blustery **seascape.** He has smudged the paint to make it look like water crashing against the sides of the boat. The smudgy marks swirl around the boat. This makes it quite difficult to see. It feels like we could really be there.

Rough Sea by Emil Nolde,
around 1920–1930

Emil Nolde has used large brush strokes to form this
stormy scene. He uses much brighter colors than
Turner in the picture on page 26. The unusual colors
create patterns. The painting shows how beautiful
Nolde thinks this display of nature is.

Weather as People

Some cultures draw weather so that it looks like people. This is called **personification.** The ancient Egyptians showed the sun as a god named Re. Re was always drawn with a **falcon** head wearing a crown made of a huge yellow or golden sun.

A wall painting of Re, the Egyptian sun god, from about 3,000 years ago

Winter by David Teniers the Younger, around 1644

The painting on the right is a personification of winter. It shows an old man warming his hands over a fire. How many things in this picture remind you of winter?

Design your own person as a type of weather condition

Instructions:

1. First, choose a type of weather. You could use snow, lightning, sun, rain, or fog.

2. Write a list of things that remind you of the weather you have chosen. These might include icicles, hats and gloves for snow, or an umbrella, rain boots, and water for rain.

3. Make a sketch of a person and add the items from your list to the design. You should now have your "weather person!"

Glossary

Aboriginal used to describe the group of people living in Australia from the earliest times, since before Europeans arrived there

background part of a picture that looks the furthest away

cold color color that make us feel cold, for example, blue or green

dramatic effect technique used to put excitement into a picture

environment natural surroundings in which plants, animals, and people live

falcon type of bird that hunts for food

foreground part of the picture that looks the nearest

illustration drawing or picture in a book

impasto thickly applied paint

Internet system that allows communication between different computer networks around the world

palette tool used by artists to mix paint on

pergola walkway covered with plants

personification idea drawn in a human form

perspective technique that artists use to give pictures a feeling of space and distance

prehistoric from earliest times, before records of events were made

sculpture piece of art made from a solid material, often stone, wood, metal, or clay

seascape picture that shows a view of the sea

studio room that an artist uses to work in

symbol picture that represents something else

texture in art, if you give something texture, you make it look how it might feel if you could touch it

warm color color that make us feel warm, for example, red, yellow, or orange

weather forecast report of what the weather is going to be like in the future

More Books to Read

Heinemann Library's **How Artists Use** series:

- *Color*
- *Line and Tone*
- *Pattern and Texture*

- *Perspective*
- *Shape*

Heinemann Library's **The Life and Work of** series:

- *Alexander Calder*
- *Auguste Rodin*
- *Buonarroti Michelangelo*
- *Claude Monet*
- *Diego Rivera*
- *Edgar Degas*
- *Frederick Remington*
- *Georges Seurat*
- *Grandma Moses*
- *Henri Matisse*
- *Henry Moore*

- *Joseph Turner*
- *Leonardo da Vinci*
- *Mary Cassatt*
- *Paul Cezanne*
- *Paul Gauguin*
- *Paul Klee*
- *Pieter Brueghel*
- *Rembrandt van Rijn*
- *Vincent van Gogh*
- *Wassily Kandinsky*

Index